No. 1 Top Book On Backpacking

Ultralight Backpacking

The only guide you need to travel light.

The best book with secret tips you need to know.

Copyright 2019

David E. King

Contents

Introduction 1

Reasons To Go Ultralight Backpacking 4

Benefits Of Ultralight Backpacking 7

Downsides Of Ultralight Backpacking 9

Essential Ultralight Backpacking Skills 11

Ultralight Backpacking Basics 15

Going Ultralight With The Big Four 17

Tips For Saving Weight Without Sacrificing Comfort 26

How To Stay Safe, Warm, Well-Fed & Happy 34

Backpacking Food Mistakes To Avoid 45

Conclusion 51

Introduction

Ultralight backpacking is a style of backpacking that emphasizes carrying the lightest and simplest gear safely possible for a given trip. Base weight (the weight of a backpack plus the gear inside & outside it, excluding consumables such as food, water, and fuel, which vary depending on the duration and style of trip) is reduced as much as safely possible, though reduction of the weight of consumables is also applied.

Although no technical standards exist, the terms light and ultralight commonly refer to backpackers and gear who achieve a base weight below 15 pounds (6.8 kg) and 10 pounds (4.5 kg) respectively in the Contiguous United States, 3 Season; elsewhere the definitions are commonly given as lightweight being under 15 kg, and ultralight under 10 kg. For comparison, traditional backpacking ppractices often results in base weights above 30 pounds (14 kg), and sometimes up to 60 pounds (27 kg).

By carrying lighter and more multi-purpose equipment, ultralight backpackers aim to cover longer distances per day with less wear and tear on the body. This is particularly useful when through-hiking a long-distance trail. Many adherents suggest the following steps (in order of weight and least cost):

Reduce each item's weight. Modifying items to reduce superfluous weight, replacing items manufactured using heavy materials with items made from lighter ones, and exchanging fully featured items for minimalist (and therefore lighter) items.[3] Based upon actual weight to be saved, one can make trades with cost, effectiveness, reliability, lifespan, etc.

Weigh everything. An implied, but often overlooked, necessity is to first weigh every item and record its weight. Only with precise before and after weights can one optimize total pack weight.

Carry less. Omit unnecessary items such as camp chairs, coffee makers, electronic gadgets, multiple items of clothing, etc.

Share gear with others. For example, four people sleep in a four-person tent, one stove for 2–4 people, etc.

Swap gear for skills through reading and practice. The greater one's skills in using the environment and gear, the fewer tools one needs to carry. For example, by knowing where exactly to find water, one needs not carry as much.

Lighten your feet. Hiking shoes are often cheaper and lighter than hiking boots.

Rethink, Reduce, and Repackage. Carry only what you'll need for that trip of fuel, sunblock, string, batteries, lotions, etc. This often means repackaging items.

Multi-purpose. Try to find items that work well for different tasks, for example a bandana, poncho + tent, hiking + tent poles, wool sock + mittens, etc.

Replace gear. Only at this last step, purchase/borrow lighter weight gear. Start with the shelter, sleeping, and carrying systems (commonly called the Big Three) which might include a tent/tarp/bivy, sleeping bag/quilt, sleeping pad, and backpack). Only last, think about a short toothbrush.

All these efforts can result in base backpacking weight that is under six pounds (3 kg). Although focusing on the pack's weight is common, the philosophy of ultralight travel applies to the person (e.g. trim vs. obese) and everything carried (e.g. skin-out weight).

Reasons To Go Ultralight Backpacking

For the most dedicated, ultralight backpacking is more than a matter of shedding excess gear. Ultralight backpacking is a way of life, an obsessive art form of shaving off pack weight down to the absolute minimum limit of necessity.

Entering into the world of ultralight backpacking will test your resourcefulness and challenge your ideas about what you need to survive. Casting off the luxuries of your daily life grants a new kind of freedom, a self-reliant pride that can only spring from forgoing the comforts of home.

Going ultralight has big benefits. With a little experience, research and DIY experimentation, you can go from lightweight to ultralight fairly easily.

What is Ultralight Backpacking?

"Ultralight backpacking" is a form of backpacking with the goal of maintaining the lightest level of gear in your pack without compromising your safety. Defining that level of gear is somewhat loose though - there's no set poundage that acts as a cutoff point. The final weight of your pack will (and should) vary according to the climate, the weather, the length of your trip and other environmental factors.

Base Weight = Total Pack Weight - Consumables

The number most associated with the weight of your pack is "base weight". Total pack weight is everything (stove, pack, sleeping bag, etc). Consumables are anything that can vary in weight on your trip (food, water, soap, toilet paper, etc).

To understand what constitutes an ultralight pack, let's take a look at some of the common classifications for pack weight.

Minimalist.

"Minimalist backpacking" is a term sometimes used to describe an even lighter form of ultralight packing. Through obsessive gear modification, spartan survival skills, and lots of ingenuity, minimalist backpackers keep their pack base weight to a scant 10 pounds or under--occasionally even dipping into single digits.

Ultralight.

Expert ultralight pack base weights usually hover around the 15 pound mark, often aiming for the low teens. However, with the latest gear, a bit of planning and favorable weather conditions, it's fairly easy for less experienced backpackers to go ultralight.

Lightweight.

Most recreational backpackers will fall into the lightweight range: around 25 pounds or so. The lightweight pack allows for a couple creature comforts alongside the essentials--a warmer sleeping bag, for example, or electronics like Kindles and phones.

Luxury.

What you see in the movies - a pack the size of Texas engulfing someone with all sorts of odds and ends tied to it. Common backpacking wisdom states your pack shouldn't exceed a 1/3 of your weight. Most hikers can pack quite a bit of luxury items and supplies before reaching this limit.

Of course, there's nothing inherently wrong with loading up your pack with the comforts of home. But if you find yourself in the "luxury" camp, it's worth considering what you actually need on the trail, and which gear you can stand to lose.

Benefits Of Ultralight Backpacking

1. More miles.

The less encumbered you are, the farther and faster you can travel. With less weight on your back, you'll be able to keep a quicker pace, covering a greater distance each day on the trail.

Your newfound, speedier pace will open up more opportunities as well. For example, a trip that might take a traditional backpacker a full week to complete can be tackled over the course of a long weekend by an ultralight hiker.

2. Efficiency.

Consider yourself an engine. The heavier your load, the more fuel it takes to get the same distance. Carrying a lighter requires less fuel - food and nutrition and your case.

3. A lighter step.

Less weight on your back means more comfort while you hike. Overall, your time on the trial will be more enjoyable the lighter your load - you'll spend less time looking at your feet and more time taking in the scenery.

4. Maneuverability.

A heavy pack can limit your mobility on the trail, forcing you to slow down to hump your pack over obstacles and tough terrain. Ultralight packs allow you to navigate rougher territory with ease and speed.

5. Reduce likelihood of injury.

Lighter packs offer relief for your bones and muscles, particularly for those who are recovering from an injury or managing a physical disability. Even those in perfect health can reduce their chance of future injury by lightening their load. Going up and down mountains with a heavy load can damage your knees, in particular.

Downsides Of Ultralight Backpacking

No luxury items.

There's no doubt that ultralight backpacking will force you to leave most of your indulgences at home. Luxury items - extra tasty food, extra clothes, extra anything - may be sorely missed.

Less comfort.

You may be forced to settle for a thinner sleeping bag, or a tarp instead of an enclosed bug proof tent. One way or another, ultralight backpacking will leave you more exposed to nature and the elements.

Flimsier gear.

In general, some ultralight gear and supplies aren't as sturdy as more conventional backpacking gear. You'll have to use extra care to avoid damaging your gear out on the trail.

More extreme conditions.

☐Inexperienced backpackers should take care not to exceed the limits of their ability. With less gear, personal experience and a bit of survival skills are crucial to ensure safety.

Essential Ultralight Backpacking Skills

Ultralight backpacking requires an extreme form of self-reliance where backpackers compensate for bringing less gear by having more advanced backcountry skills. While many other backpackers and day hikers have these same skills, "going ultralight," or the less extreme "lightweight" is more committing, since ultralight backpackers carry less navigational, comfort, and convenience items in their packs.

For instance, if gear weight considerations make it infeasible to carry a GPS w/ extra batteries or a shelter with a built-in floor, you need to be able to compensate by using lightweight navigation tools like map and compass and possess better campsite selection skills to offset adverse weather.

1. Trip Planning

Detailed trip planning is the most important skill that ultralight backpackers should cultivate. Planning a trip requires a lot more than just deciding where to go and when. It usually requires researching seasonal weather conditions, planning a route, estimating travel times, addressing logistic issues such as transportation and resupply points, determining water availability, identifying hazardous plants or wildlife, learning new skills you will need, assessing your physical fitness relative to your distance goals, group management considerations, contingency planning, and risk management.

2. Equipment and Clothing Selection

Once you've planned the route and environmental requirements of your journey, you can select the clothing and equipment required. If the gear you own doesn't satisfy your trip requirements, you may have to buy more appropriate clothing and equipment or change your route to lower your level of risk.

3. Thermoregulation

In order to plan the right clothing for a trip, you need to understand how your body reacts to the temperatures and weather you are likely encounter, and how your metabolism, clothing selection, and activity level can be used regulate your body temperature. Called thermoregulation, it takes practice to understand how to regulate your metabolism and dress to prevent hypothermia or heat related illness.

4. Campsite Selection

Ultralight tents and shelters are less weather resistant than heavier three season tents. Good campsite selection and orientation skills can identify campsites that are better protected from the wind, cold air pockets, or groundwater, while minimizing your impact on plant life and animals.

5. Nutrition and Food Preparation

The heaviest item in an ultralight backpacker's pack is likely to be food. Eliminating excess packaging and knowing how to select foods high in calories and nutritional value can lower the weight of your food bag significantly.

6. Weather and Environmental Awareness

Weather changes can have a greater impact on ultralight backpackers depending on the shelter and amount of clothing they carry. It's important therefore to develop an awareness to changing weather conditions and take mitigating actions. Seeking shelter, forest cover, or changing your route can reduce exposure to high winds, hail, heavy rain, or other environmental factors such as flash floods or forest fires.

7. On-Trail and Off-Trail Navigation

On trail and off-trail routes often require different levels of navigational expertise, but being proficient using the simplest tools, such as map and compass, can eliminate the need to carry much heavier navigational aids such as GPS units and the extra batteries or power packs that they require.

8. Survival Skills and Wilderness First Aid

Solid survival skills and wilderness first aid enable one to use natural features and resources to compensate for the lack of gear in survival situations. While these skills are taught for use in emergencies, they can also be used to increase your comfort when the weather or conditions exceed the capabilities of the ultralight gear you've decided to bring on your trip.

9. Gear Maintenance and Repair

Ultralight backpacking gear can be quite fragile and must be treated with care to make it last. This can include field repairs such as fixing a broken zipper or sewing torn fabric, which can put gear or clothing out of action, unless you can patch it up on the spot.

Ultralight Backpacking Basics

By the 1960s, a century later, backpackers were carrying up to 50 or even 70 pounds' worth of gear. In the 1990s, the mindset began to change and modern materials have swung the pendulum back to the "less is more" philosophy.

So, what is ultralight backpacking? No official definition of "ultralight" exists. It's more a frame of mind than an arbitrary pack weight. It's about deciding you can get by with less. You can find your own sweet spot on a continuum of, say, 12 to 28 pounds. Relying less on gear means relying more on your own judgment of how to stay safe, healthy and comfortable on the trail.

If you're ready to lighten your load on the trail, here are a few tips for starters:

Weigh your gear: Find a kitchen and/or luggage scale and weigh your current gear. Make a note of your current "base weight": everything on your back except food, water and fuel (known as consumables).

Replace older gear with lighter gear: As you replace old gear and choose new gear, pay close attention to each item's weight. You'll be aiming for a total base weight of about 10 pounds. (Once you add consumables that weight may double.)

Make gradual changes: Because gear can be more expensive the lighter it gets, a smart approach may be to lessen your load over time. Replace one "big ticket" item at a time with a lighter-weight (and potentially more costly) model.

Understand the tradeoffs: Sewing your own pack and other gear, as many do, is a great way to go lighter and save money. Keep in mind that while lighter in weight, ultralight gear may not be as durable or as comfortable in the long run as conventional gear.

Going Ultralight With The Big Four

The fastest way to lighten your load is to replace one or all of the four largest items most backpackers carry: pack, tent, sleeping bag and pad.

Backpack

While a traditional backpacker might have a 65-liter pack in the three- to four-pound range, savvy ultralight devotees may choose a frameless, minimally-padded 45- to 55-liter pack, occasionally even smaller, weighing a scant one-and-a-half to two pounds.

Shelter

Tents: If you prefer the cozy feel of a tent, choose a full-mesh tent (with rainfly) to keep out insects and other small critters. You can find an ultralight one-person tent (using a trekking pole for support) at around one pound; two pounds is more common.

Tarps: You can create a decent rain shelter out of an ultralight tarp. It may require guylines and a couple trees, stakes or trekking poles for support.

Bivy sacks. These generally weigh between one and two pounds for a waterproof shell; a bare-minimum bag may weigh about six ounces.

Ultralight hammocks, which may include a bug net or rainfly, are also becoming a popular choice.

Sleeping bag

Choose down—it's lighter and more compressible than synthetic fill. Most down now is treated to be water-resistant. You can find a down bag weighing one or two pounds.

To lower your bag weight:

- Choose a bag no warmer than you really need. Extra warmth just means extra weight.
- Choose a mummy bag without a hood; wear a balaclava and/or warm knit hat on cold nights.
- Consider a down trekking quilt (becoming popular with thru-hikers) instead of a sleeping bag.

Sleeping pad

Air pads have replaced self-inflating pads as the lightest comfort pads for backpacking. For under one pound you can get a full-length pad that offers a lot of cushioning and even a little insulation. Thru-hikers, however, still typically prefer a closed-cell foam pad for their greater durability over the long haul.

To save ounces, choose a torso-length pad, or you can cut down a closed-cell foam pad. You can use your pack under your feet for insulation from the ground, but here's where your comfort decision comes into play.

Water, Fuel and Food

After the big four, these are your heaviest items. Learn to carry only as much as you need for the length of time you'll be on the trail.

Water

You don't need to carry all the water you'll need for the entire day. Do your research and find out where streams and lakes are found along your route so you can filter and refill along the way. Some tips:

- "Camel up" before you leave camp each morning by drinking a good amount of water. Do the same each time you reach a water source (after you filter, of course). This way you may find you can get by with carrying less water as you hike.
- Carry only one liter (2.2 pounds) if that seems feasible (unless you're in a desert, then you'll need more) between water sources.
- Carry a mini filter (some weigh only two ounces) and some backup purification tablets (in a tiny plastic bag, not the glass bottle they may come in).

- Use collapsible water bottles (One- to two-liter capacity). A soft bottle is 80 percent lighter than a hard-plastic water bottle.

Fuel, Stove and Cookware

To stay light, plan to simply boil water to add to dehydrated food instead of cooking a meal from scratch. This saves weight both on the food and the fuel. Regarding cookware, think dual-purpose: a titanium mug can also serve as a pot. Bring a spork instead of a spoon and a fork.

Popular ultralight stove options:

Tablet fuel stoves: You can make the stove out of an aluminum can or buy one, and bring a tablet of fuel per day or per meal, as you figure out your needs.

Alcohol stove: Weighs a mere ounce. Bring a bottle containing only as many fluid ounces of alcohol as you'll need per meal per person per day. Make sure the bottle is sturdy enough not to puncture or break inside your pack (keep it inside a zip-top bag just in case)

Canister stove: These tiny folding stoves may weigh only two- to three ounces. However, they screw onto isobutane canisters that weigh quite a bit. Learn through practice how many meals you can get out of one canister. A rule of thumb is two ounces per day (that's enough for one person eating two meals each day).

Integrated canister stove system Yes, some ultralight backpackers will bring one of these, especially for two or more people. While heavier, this system boils water very quickly so you may save weight by bringing less fuel.

Food. Plan on bringing enough food to give you 3,000 to 4,000 calories per day, or about two pounds of food per day, depending on how many miles you cover and how fast, and how strenuous the elevation gain/loss is.

Some ultralight food tips:

Go instant: For breakfast, instant coffee and instant oatmeal are quick and fuel-efficient. On cold mornings, eat a protein bar to get up and moving in the morning; stop later along the trail for your oatmeal. Be calorie conscious: Bring fat- and calorie-rich snacks for lunch: protein bars, nuts, seeds, chocolate, dried fruit, powder supplements, and if you don't mind the weight, some hard cheese and salami.

Dehydrate your own food at home. This saves money and packaging, plus you get to create and season meals the way you like.

Do your own packaging: Store each dried dinner in a zip-top freezer bag and add your hot water directly to it (the bag can withstand near-boiling water).

Rehydrate some foods using cold water and letting sit for an hour or two; this saves fuel.

Use what you find, first: If you do eat out of a mug or pot and need to clean it beyond a mere rinse, use leaves, sand or grass to wipe out the vessel first. Then use a bit of water and scrub if necessary with a one-by-two-inch piece of sponge (cut from a larger one at home).

Additional Ultralight Backpacking Tips

Don't skimp on safety: As you lower weight, keep in mind that every time you step into the backcountry, you should pack the Ten Essentials. While it's smart to pack light, it's equally smart to pack safely.

Navigation system: Bring a map, compass, and a GPS watch or device. Learn about the pros and cons of a personal locator beacon with satellite messaging. These are heavy, but can give you (and your loved ones at home) peace of mind knowing you can send "I'm fine" messages or summon help.

Safety whistle: A lightweight yet loud whistle can be worn around your neck so it's ready to use in an emergency. Three blasts is the international distress call for help.

Sun protection: Bring a few ounces of sunscreen in a small bottle and a tube of lip balm rated UPF 30. A good sun-shading hat is your first line of defense. In the desert, consider hiking in sun gloves and a UPF 50+ long-sleeve shirt. Sunglasses are a necessity for good eye health.

Illumination: Find a no-frills, low-weight kids' or adult headlamp weighing two or three ounces including batteries. Put in fresh batteries right before you leave home so you don't have to bring extras (depending on length of trip). You can even light up your camp with a small LED lantern that weighs 2.5 ounces including its single AA battery. To go truly minimalist, use only tiny LED microlights that weigh 0.5 ounce.

Insulation and clothing: Always carry a lightweight down or synthetic puffy jacket. For base layers, you'll want long underwear bottoms and usually a long-sleeve top as well. Many long-distance backpackers swear by running shorts with built-in underwear; bring long pants if any scrambling on your route is expected. Bringing two pairs of wool or synthetic underwear (wear one, wash one). Two or three pairs of wool or synthetic socks seems to work well for most ultralight backpackers.

Rain/storm gear: This includes your rain jacket, rain pants, warm hat and gloves, pack cover (or internal trash bag), and optional waterproof rain mitts. Keep these at the top of your pack for quick access should you need them quickly.

Bandana: This clothing item is so versatile it's worth a special mention. Wear it as a headband, a sun cape under a cap or a damp cooling cloth around your neck. Or use it as a towel for dishes or drying your body, a pot holder, or even a bandage or tourniquet in an emergency. Women, bring a dedicated one for a pee rag.

Footwear: Most ultralight backpackers wear light hikers or trail-running shoes. Before you make the switch from sturdy boots, strengthen your feet on load-bearing day hikes. Many hikers swear by non-waterproof footwear as it dries more quickly.

Scaled-down first-aid kit and repair kit: Bring a few of the following: blister pads, gauze pads, bandages, antibiotic ointment in tiny packets, pain-relief pills, and a razor blade (can take the place of a knife or scissors in your pack). Bring a few inches of duct tape wrapped around a water bottle or lighter. A piece of gear-repair tape is also useful in case you get a hole in your pack, sleeping bag or air pad.

Cleaning and hygiene: Here's a minimal amount of things to bring in order to help stay healthy on the trail:

Small bottle of hand sanitizer to use after going to the bathroom and before preparing meals.

Travel-size tube of toothpaste (squeeze out half to use at home); or baking soda in a baggie that you can moisten with water.

Toothbrush cut in half, or child-size toothbrush.

Small bottle or piece of biodegradable soap (for cleaning your hands and body outside of camp, never in a water source)

Two pre-moistened wipes per day (one for hands, neck and face; one for your nether regions). At home, take your allotted wipes and leave them out overnight to dry a bit. This lowers their weight. Put them in a zip-top bag. Remoisten if needed with a bit of filtered water on the trail. Wipes need to be packed out, not buried, as most contain plastic.

Two squares of toilet paper per day. Use heavy-duty paper towels cut into 4-inch squares in place of regular toilet paper. Or measure out wads of regular toilet paper and leave the rest on the cardboard at home. Put the paper in a zip-top bag. Carry a zip-top waste bag to pack out.

Pee rag for women: a quarter of a full-size bandana works well; tie onto outside of pack for drying.

Backpacking trowel: Consider bringing an ultralight one for digging your cat hole. Wipe first with soft leaves or smooth stones or sticks, then use a square or two of paper.

Trekking poles: Choose carbon fiber for the lightest weight. Poles are invaluable for maintaining balance on rocky terrain, alleviating knee strain on uphills and downhills, and serving as shelter poles.

Luxury items: Every ultralight hiker brings at least one thing that makes their trip a little more pleasant. It could be a pair of small binoculars if you're a birder, or a journal to take notes in. Allow yourself a treat or two for the trail.

Tips For Saving Weight Without Sacrificing Comfort

These ultralight backpacking tips focus on easy, practical changes you can make to shed weight while still being comfortable and having durable gear on the trail.

Focus on Items with Multiple Uses

Take a look at every item in your backpack and make sure you know how to maximize its use. Many items you carry on backpacking trips can have more than one use.

- A cooking pot can be used as a bowl

- A stuff sack can double as a pillow once you stuff your down jacket into it
- A bandana can cool you down on hot days, provide shade, serve as a makeshift coffee filter. In an emergency, it can also be a tourniquet
- Pants that roll up or zipper off into shorts are great for versatility and sudden weather changes. When prepping for a trip, try to switch out super specific items with multi-purpose items wherever possible.

Cut the Non-Essentials

Did you really need a coffee mug AND a stainless steel cup for wine? Set out your gear before heading out and check to see if you can eliminate at least 1-2 items. Then, after each backpacking trip, create a list of everything in your pack that you didn't use. If an item keeps reappearing on this list, CUT IT.

With that being said, first aid and emergency equipment is essential and is an exception to this rule. You can, however, make sure that your first aid kit isn't overkill; this Ultralight Adventure Medical Kit weighs only 3.7 ounces and has the essentials for dealing with minor injuries.

When packing your clothes for the backcountry, be minimal but prepared. Do you need a new outfit each day? Probably not, and keep in mind sweaty clothes can be even heavier to carry than clean clothes. You can generally only wear one base layer, one mid layer and one insulating layer at a time, so duplicates aren't necessary unless you are hiking somewhere with extreme weather where you need a backup. Packing lightweight rain protection can help ensure you stay dry as well. Only pack spares of socks and underwear.

Shed Weight on the "Big Three"

Going lightweight can be EXPENSIVE, but you don't need to completely makeover your entire gear closet. If you want to make small changes that will have big impacts on your pack weight, start with the big three:

Your tent, sleeping bag, & pack

While high quality, lightweight versions of these items can be an investment, once you have them you should be set for years. If you're in the market for new ultralight backpacking gear, you should also keep an eye out for sales that happen at REI throughout the year. REI's Anniversary Sale in May, right after the annual dividends are distributed, is a great time to purchase big-ticket items since you can save sometimes 30% or more.

YOUR TENT

On average, 2-person backpacking tents today weigh about 2-3 pounds, and every year they seem to get lighter as technology improves. First, consider how many people you'll be camping with. If you sleep solo when you backpack, then opt for a 1-man tent. If you already have a two-man tent, then share your space with a friend or your partner, and then have the benefit of being able to split up the weight.

Next, ask what kind of weather you'll be backpacking in most frequently. If you tend to hike in warm, sunny environments, you might consider an ultralight backpacking tarp shelter like the Sea to Summit Escapist Tarp Shelter that utilizes your trekking poles as tent poles. Just make sure you practice setting up your tent before you leave your house since it takes a little skill.

If it rains a lot where you backpack, then you'll want something a little burlier that can handle wind and inclement weather. Luckily there are still a lot of good ultralight backpacking tent options that are still really durable, like the NEMO Hornet 2p Tent.

SLEEPING BAG

High-quality, lightweight sleeping bags will often positively impact you in more ways than shedding pack weight; they also pack down to a minimal size. For your sleeping bag, aim to stay below 3 pounds so that with a 1 pound sleeping pad, you'll be right at 4 pounds for both. Quilts are also a great lightweight option if it's not too cold where you backpack.

Generally warmer sleeping bags weigh more (and cost more) because they need more fill to insulate you from the cold. This means you should think about the temperatures you'll be camping at before investing in a bag. There's no need to carry a zero degree bag if you are backpacking in warmer summer temps. My favorite ultralight backpacking sleeping bag that is an excellent compromise between warmth, weight AND price is the REI Joule sleeping bag (for women) & the REI Igneo (for men). I took the REI Joule on the John Muir Trail and loved it. For extra space savings in your backpack, stuff your sleeping bag in an ultralight compression sack.

BACKPACKING PACK

People often forget that their physical pack, even when empty, weighs something. I've been backpacking with the Deuter Aircontact Pack, and while I find it very comfortable, the pack weighs a whopping 6 pounds! Alternatively, ultralight backpacking packs built for thru-hikers barely weigh 2 pounds. These ultralight packs have a smaller capacity and are made for smaller loads. Choosing one of these packs forces you to commit to ultralight backpacking since they become uncomfortable if you try to carry loads more than 35-40 pounds. Kim used a ULA backpacking pack on her PCT hike, and loved it. One ultralight backpacking brand I've had my eye on that is very popular with thru-hikers is Granite Gear. The Granite Gear 60 liter Womens Crown2 pack and the mens version weigh just over 2 pounds, are rated for 35 pounds and have fully adjustable hip belts, lids, and a number of other features. They also cost about $200 which is less expensive than a lot of heavier backpacks.

Think in Terms of Ounces

It's all about ounces when talking about lightweight backpacking. Don't use averages or estimates – know the weight in ounces of every item in your pack, especially when you are purchasing new gear. "About" 2 pounds doesn't cut it; is it really 2 pounds OR 2 pounds AND 5 ounces. If you want to get serious about ultralight backpacking, a bathroom or luggage scale will help you with weighing gear. Weigh everything in your pack and get down to the nitty gritty because all those extra ounces add up quickly.

Choose Smart Materials

Titanium is expensive, but it's lightweight and durable. Synthetic layers are lighter than cotton and are better for hiking because they dry quickly and wick the sweat off your body. This means that rather than bringing a bunch of extra clothing, you can hang out your shirt for an hour and it will be dry and ready for the next day (unless you're hiking somewhere extra cold in the winter, then I wouldn't recommend this strategy). Just make sure to bring a set of warm, dry clothes to change into in the evening. Research the gear you are buying so you know if it's both lightweight AND a material that will last.

Get Organized

Keep a list of everything in your pack and its weight. We know this sounds a little intense but when you physically see how fast all your gear weight adds up it helps. Lay everything out before it goes into your pack so you can see what you'll be carrying. If you have a pack with numerous pockets, have an organization system for what goes where. Being organized will help prevent you from bringing things you don't need and throwing in extra items on your way out the door just because you have the room in your pack.

Don't Carry More Water than you Need

Water is likely one of the heaviest things you'll be carrying. Find out where on the trail you can expect to find water and then plan to carry the appropriate amount of water based on that. It's always a good idea to get updated trail information from the local ranger station or a recent trail report before heading out because you don't want to find out that the creek you expected to be there is completely dried up. Carry multiple bottles instead of one giant bottle so you can distribute the weight on either side of your pack. We like the tall, slender 1 liter SmartWater bottles since they can fit in the slimmest of side pockets or collapsible water bottles that get smaller as you drink. You can also save on weight by choosing purification drops and a bandana to filter sediment vs a water filter.

Make Healthy Choices

People sometimes focus relentlessly on cutting ounce after ounce off of their packs, yet they don't consider the weight they are already carrying on their own two feet. Being fit and healthy before heading out on the trail will make your overall experience more enjoyable. A backpacking trip is a great motivation for squeezing in some training hikes and eating healthy to ensure you're fit for the trail.

Plan Your Food Strategically

Food weighs ALOT. Plus it's one of the easiest things to overpack. I can't tell you how many times I've gone backpacking with wayyyyy too much food. Before you head out on your trip, try to lay out your food meal by meal for each day of your trip. This will help you visualize whether you are bringing too much or not enough. If you start with too much, you can then take away the heaviest of your food off your packing list.

Research lightweight backpacking food options that are still high in calories and protein. While fresh fruit sounds great on the trail, you can pack twice as much dried fruit in the same space, for less weight, and then you don't have to pack out food waste (such as orange peels and apple cores). While eating fresh is always preferred, when I'm on the trail, I opt for dehydrated backpacker meals. They take up so little room in your pack, weigh less than anything you might cook from scratch, and the convenience makes them all the more satisfying.

Dehydrated backpacker meals can be expensive, but when you compare to all of the ingredients you have to buy if you want to cook from scratch, plus the hassle of doing dishes, it makes it worth it to me. Another tip, if you purchase your backpacker food at REI, you save 10% when you purchase 8 or more meals at a time. Even if you don't need 8 for your upcoming trip, these backpacker meals last for a long time, so it pays to buy in bulk. Then you'll have them on hand when you want to plan a spontaneous backpacking trip.

If you're serious about going ultralight and are only going out for a night or two, you can also consider ditching the stove and fuel and eating snacks for all of your meals, which will save you a pound or two.

Keep Learning

Set a goal to learn something new with every hike you take. Look for more helpful articles, and talk to others on the trail to learn their tips and tricks for keeping weight low. You can even take a class. Your expertise will continue to grow and your pack weight will reduce with each backpacking trip you take!

And remember….it's not a competition. When I was on the John Muir Trail, I heard people constantly comparing their pack weight which drove me nuts. It's not about who has the lightest pack. It's about finding the sweet spot between being comfortable while you're hiking and comfortable at camp. Everyone has a different threshold, and the more you backpack, the more you'll learn about what YOU do and don't need to have an enjoyable hike.

How To Stay Safe, Warm, Well-Fed & Happy

An ultralight backpack means more fun. Enjoy floating down the trail instead of hauling heavy gear. You can have an ultralight backpack if you mercilessly analyze every piece of gear in your pack. Here are 201 tips to consider for reducing the weight of your pack. Some are big, some are small. That's part of the secret. Small things add up. The old and obvious are mentioned because they are some of the most important. Have fun being a fanatic. If your friends make negative comments, invite them to lift your pack and compare it to theirs. Think of these tips as a buffet, and take what you like:

Good camping skills:

Good camping skills are the key to staying warm, dry and happy while backpacking ultralight. Having confidence in your camping skills, means that you won't compensate by packing a bunch of heavy over-kill gear and backup gear. As an example, a surprising number of AT solo hikers, who sleep 95% of the time in shelters, still insist on carrying a 4-6lb., two-person, four-season dome tent instead of bringing a ½-pound tarp for the occasional times they might sleep outside of a shelter—even in June. By camping skills, I mean the common skills that every backpacker probably knows how to do (or should know)—not the questionable survival "skills" of reality TV. Here are some of what I believe are the most important skills:

Campsite selection:

While those Backpacker Magazine and calendar photos of tents at beautiful campsites on the bare shore of a stunning alpine lake, or high on some slickrock outcrop in Utah look tempting… they are horrible places to be in stormy weather—even in a tent. You will be unnecessarily at risk when your shelter is exposed, unprotected to the full force of winds and precipitation of a storm.   So pitch your shelter (tent, tarp, or pyramid) in a protected area, a few hundred feet above the lowest area, preferably in trees while backpacking ultralight. Trees do a number of lovely things for you:

- Discreetly camping out of sight in the trees, is a favor to others sharing the area with you—rather than advertising your presence to everybody for miles around.

- Trees provide wonderful anchors for tarps, shelter tie-outs, and hammocks.
- They block the wind, which keeps you a lot warmer (reduces convective heat loss). It also lowers wind load and stresses on your shelter and tent stakes.
- Trees prevent radiant heat loss. They reflect the day's heat back to the ground at night in the same way that a cloudy sky makes it warmer overnight.

Camping in the trees is also less prone to the heavy dew and condensation of exposed campsites. The worst place for dew is in a treeless meadow at the bottom of a canyon. The best place to be is in the woods on a flat area a few hundred feet above the canyon bottom (or surrounding lower area).

Know how to pitch your shelter:

- Be solid on this before your trip. It's not rocket science. Anybody can pitch a tarp or pyramid shelter with just a bit of effort.
- Read and follow the manufacturer's instructions. They are likely excellent.
- Setup your shelter in the backyard, or nearby park/playing field a few times before you go. If you are backpacking with a partner do this together. You should be able to easily pitch a tarp or pyramid shelter in 3 to 5 minutes.
- For a basic tarp, there's no need to get fancy. An A-frame pitch between two trekking poles (or better, two trees) will work fine 95% of the time. In strong winds, pitch it lower to the ground and flatter.

- Orient your shelter to the expected wind direction. Orient tarps with the narrower/rear end low and into the wind, pyramid shelters/tents with the door facing away from the wind.

In very strong winds, use the the additional tie-out points on your shelter.

Use sturdy Y-stakes. They have great holding power, and you can pound them into rocky ground. Always carry 1-2 spare stakes and a few hanks of spare cord.

Shelter cord adjusters can slip. Know a few basic knots and guyline management—a figure 8 loop at the end of a line, girth hitch and a trucker's hitch for guyline tension adjustment.

Keep hiking when it's cold:

- Moderate but consistent movement (it needn't be at all tiring or strenuous) is the key to keeping warm when it's really cold.
- Even walking 1 to 1.5 miles per hour should keep your internal, metabolic heater going, and keep your hands and feet warm. If you are getting tired you are going too fast!
- Minimize stops to essential needs, and don't make them longer than necessary. You get cold quickly, and it takes a long time to warm up again. If you're starting to chill it's time to move.
- If you really need to stop for a longer time (over 5 minutes), try to do it in a warmer, more protected area and put on warm clothing (e.g. down jacket) as soon as you stop. Take your warm clothing off just before you start hiking again.

Clothing adjustments:

Put on just enough clothing to keep you warm when moving. Overdressing, getting hot and then sweating out while backpacking ultralight is a great way to get wet and then really cold. It's very easy to get clothing wet, but it takes a long time to dry it out in cold and damp weather. Wet clothing is cold clothing and unhappiness.

Only add warmer clothing when you can no longer stay warm walking at a comfortable pace.

Note: I have a lot of experience staying warm and comfortable into the 20's F when hiking at my own pace, wearing just a 6 oz base layer, a 7 oz fleece shirt (mid-layer), a 2 oz fleece hat, and 2 oz gloves, even with some wind. [Although my warm down jacket comes out mightily fast at stops!]

Bring Light gear appropriate for the conditions

I am going to be blunt. Some gear is outright better than other gear. My light/ultralight gear, by almost every measure, outperforms the similar conventional (heavy) gear recommended by "trusted experts." E.g. compared to a 2½ pound synthetic bag rated to only +30; my one-pound, down quilt rated at +20 F is almost ⅓ the weight, warmer, far more compressible, and will last years longer. That is, I am warmer and more comfortable for ⅓ the weight. Even the cost is not much more; $250 for my down quilt vs. $160 for the synthetic sleeping bag.

Don't take extra/backup gear:

This is the easiest way to save weight and money. I only bring the right gear that I trust to work. As such, I bring few if any "backup clothes or equipment."

One thing that naturally follows from this is, "don't bring more clothing than you can wear at one time."

Your tent doesn't keep you warm: Your tent just keeps the wind and rain off—so will a tarp or pyramid shelter. What keeps you warm is a puffy down sleeping bag and jacket.

Get down:

Down is your best friend when it comes to staying warm. At a minimum get a good down sleeping bag (or quilt), and a down jacket.

Don't believe the dire warnings about getting down wet—it's really hard to do. In over 40 years of backpacking all over the world in all sorts of conditions, I have yet to get my down so wet that it didn't do a good job of keeping me warm. New water resistant shell fabrics and water resistant down only improve upon this.

The only advantage to synthetics is price, and then only in the short term. In the long term I find they usually lose loft after less than a season of use. This makes them a poor long term value. A good down bag will easily last 5 to 10 years.

And make no mistake, a wet synthetic sleeping bag or jacket is no joy! Keeping your gear dry is a better strategy for both down and synthetic gear.

Bring a sleeping bag for the average temp:

I bring a sleeping bag (or quilt) rated for the average expected low temperature for the area and time of year I am backpacking. If I get a period of unexpectedly cold weather (it happens), I supplement my sleeping bag with my fleece mid-layer, down jacket, warm hat (and down pants and booties if I have them).

Extra shirts, pants and base-layers are a poor choice to stay warm:

Your money and gear weight is better spent on buying a warmer down bag and jacket. Or even down pants, down hat and down booties.

And one 6-10 oz fleece/wool mid layer garment is all you need

Get a weather report:

The NOAA hourly weather graph is among the most informative and accurate.

Then pack for those conditions! Since 90% of backpackers take 90% of their trips for three days or less, this weather report should be quite accurate for the short time you are out.

This will let you pack a shelter, clothing, and sleeping bag appropriate for actual conditions.

It will also deter you from taking fear-based, "what-if-the-worst-happens!" gear, e.g. a 6 pound tent, a +10F sleeping bag, and a down jacket for a warm weather trip on the Appalachian Trail.

For longer term gear planning there is historical average weather Data on Accuweather which will help you intelligently select gear months before your trip.

In summary: the historical average weather will assist you buying gear in advance of your trips (20 degree vs 40 degree bag, etc.). And just before your trip, the 3 day forecast/NOAA hourly weather graph should help you fine tune the gear you actually take.

Keep your gear dry:

The best way to keep your gear dry is not to get it wet in the first place. This means putting on your rainwear before you get wet. Not sweating out your clothes with perspiration while hiking. And keeping the gear in your pack dry (especially your down bag, and down jacket).

When using the pack in conjunction with stowing my sleeping bag/quilt and down jacket, I don't need to do anything different when it rains; I can just keep hiking. So my backpack is always packed the same, regardless of weather. No messing around taking on and off pack covers (imperfect rain protection anyway) or fussing with pack liners, both of which are a pain and waste of time.

If rain is possible, keep your rainwear quickly accessible in an outside pocket of your pack (I use the center rear pocket). That way you can put it on quickly, and not have to expose the main pocket of your pack to rain.

A tarp or pyramid shelter may be drier than a tent: Many times the small, confined, and less ventilated area inside a tent can be wetter than a larger (and much lighter) pyramid shelter or tarp. This is also a recommendation to buy the larger tarp or pyramid shelter. For just a little more weight you get a lot more living space!

Condensation is a big problem in small tents. It's very easy to get your gear wet from the high humidity inside. In tight quarters it's almost impossible not to brush your sleeping bag or down jacket against condensing tent walls. And if you happen to get into the tent with wet gear it is unlikely to dry in the humid climate.

In contrast, a tarp or pyramid shelter might have twice the room and be better ventilated and less humid.

And if you're stuck in the shelter for an extended period of time, you'll welcome the larger and less constricted living area of a large tarp or pyramid shelter. During long rains, small backpacking tents become more like coffins than dwellings!

Bring Nutritious high-calorie foods

You can save a lot of weight and even money by selecting the right backpacking food. My nutritious and high calorie Backpacking Food gives me 3,000 healthful and filling calories of complex carbs, protein and healthy fats for around 1.5 pound/day. Over a 3 day weekend backpacking trip I get as many calories and as much nutrition, possibly more than someone carrying almost double the food weight.

Save food weight:

My three days of food at 1.5 lbs per day = 4.5 pounds vs. the standard "recommendation" for a 3 day trip: 3 days at 2 lb food per day + 1 day backup food = 8 pounds

1.5 lbs of my food = 3,000 calories (my food is 2,000 calories per pound)

2.0 lbs of regular backpacking food = 2,800 calories (~1,400 calories per pound)

Maintain nutrition:

Try to get the most calories per unit weight in your food but not at the expense of a poor diet. You want a balanced diet with good protein, carbohydrates, healthy fats, fiber, vitamins and other nutrients.

I take unsweetened, dried fruit, freeze dried vegetables, nuts, homemade gorp, whole grain crackers, whole grain pasta, healthier-higher-calorie trail bars, and lean jerky and powdered milk and powdered soy for my protein.

See my Backpacking Food Page for more examples of healthy backpacking foods.

Don't carry extra food:

The standard advice to carry an extra day of food is hooey. I figure I can make it at least 3 days without any food. I've had to do this before and feel comfortable with my choice. Some mainstream outdoor training courses (NOLS, Outward Bound) have two to three food-less days in their programs. This is not a recommendation for others to do the same. You'll have to make your own decision on extra food. Maybe you will just bring a bit less extra food next trip. Again, think carefully about packing for "the worst case scenario".

"Skip" one day of food: I eat a big breakfast or lunch before I start hiking the first day and I eat a big meal when I get out. By boosting my off-trail calories on the first and last day I eliminate carrying a whole day's worth of food in my pack. So for a weekend trip (three days and two nights) I might carry 3.4 pounds or less of food.

Drink when thirsty and carry less water: I carry only the water I need to meet my thirst. This means I rarely carry more than a liter and usually a lot less.

"If you are thirsty, it's already too late" and "If your urine is yellow, you are dehydrated," are myths! My article The Best Hydration – Drink When Thirsty is based on the current best science (from experts in the field of sports hydration not beholden to sports drink and bottled water companies). It suggests that "drinking to thirst" is the safest and healthiest strategy for hydration during exercise. It turns out that your body's natural thirst mechanism works well to keep you hydrated and healthy during exercise. In fact, the amount of water your body requires is probably far less than what the Sports Drink and Bottled Water companies have been telling us.

Backpacking Food Mistakes To Avoid

When it comes to trip planning, backpacking food is one of the easiest things to mess up. Beginners are prone to epic mistakes. For example, I once packed five pounds of pancake mix. Don't ask. And intermediate and experienced backpackers often fall into sub-optimal packing routines simply out of laziness or lack of time. Are you dissatisfied with your adventure fuel, hoping to lighten your load, or just looking to improve an important backcountry skill? Below are 10 backpacking food mistakes and how to correct them.

But first, what makes a good backpacking diet? I believe there are six key traits: lightweight, calorie dense, low volume, varied (in flavor and texture), reasonably healthy, and easy to eat/prepare. Beyond those, you should also strive for food that tastes good, and supports your daily mileage and itinerary goals.

#1: Not enough variety

My dream backpacking meal plan consists entirely of unique food items, with no two snacks being the same. While I may never achieve that perfectly, I belive variety makes everything taste better. If you've ever been on a longer trip and packed the same things to eat every day, you'll understand the soul-crushing feeling of looking into a food bag and realizing that you already hate all the options. One way to correct this is to buy a wide variety of foods in bulk at the start of backpacking season, then store them well and dip into each for one or two serving per trip.

#2: Too much trail mix, too many bars

The most common way to fail the variety test is by overpacking in these two specific categories. I shudder to recall the times I've seen my partners snack game consisting exclusively of bars and nut mixes. Every bulk, health and junk food section will offer a wide variety of good snack options that are not those. Especially Trader Joe's, if you have them around. For maximum salivation, I personally recommend no more than one bar and two trail mixes per day.

Here are a few of my personal favorites: Half Pops, peanut butter filled pretzels, sesame sticks, Aztec trail mix, toasted coconut, dried cherries, dried mango, cinnamon candied almonds, white chocolate pretzels, Korean BBQ flavored dried chick peas, chipotle smoked gouda, Twix, fiber supplement brownies, mozzarella cheese sticks, fig newtons, salted sunflower seeds, Clif Kid Z fruit ropes, landjäger.

#3: Not enough salty food

Hiking is a sweaty business, especially in summer, and you're going to need to maintain a steady intake of electrolytes. You'll be especially hard pressed to find salts if you fall for Mistake #2. Plus, who—besides 6-year-olds—wants to eat sugary food literally all day long? To correct this, while laying out your food at home, make sure to pair each sugary snack with a savory snack and you'll guarantee an even mix.

#4: Too bulky

We only have so much room in our backpacks, so it's important to bring things that don't absorb all the space. There are three common worst offenders: hard-sided or inflated packaging, freeze-dried meals and fluffy stuff (bagels, bread, popcorn, etc). To solve this problem, make sure to decant all your food into sandwich-sized Ziploc bags, learn to pre-make your own dinners, and shop space-consciously (i.e. tortillas over bread).

#5: Too much food

Packing the exact right amount of food is exceedingly difficult and most people prefer to err on the side of caution and overpack. Often to the detriment of our legs. On numerous occasions, I've exited the trail with an entire extra day's worth of munchies. To correct for this, learn how many calories your body requires on short, medium and long hiking days, and use nutrition labels to pack approximately the right amount according to your itinerary. For the average hiker, I recommend ~3000-4000 calories on <10 mile days, ~4000-5000 on 10-20 mile days, and ~5000-6000 on 20+ mile days.

#6: Overpacking the last day's food

Speaking of overpacking, the most common way to screw up is packing too much food on the last day of the trip. Having learned this lesson, I rarely pack more than a breakfast, instead relying on consuming any overage from other days of the trip, plus fueling up immediately after with a monstrous brunch or burrito. Most people end their trip with a half day plus a drive, so unless your itinerary differs, I recommend keeping your end-game victuals to a minimum.

#7: Too little food

Beginners rarely pack too little food (see Mistake #6). This problem usually comes from the fast-and-light crowd, looking to cover maximum distance with minimal packs. That's all good and fine, but if you've ever run out of food, you know the risk-to-reward-ratio just isn't worth it. To prevent this problem while going ultralight, make sure you lay out your daily rations while packing at home, count calories, and focus on super rich options like meat, oil, cheeses, nuts, and seeds.

#8: No veggies

Most people desire to eat a complete diet, but when it comes to fruits and veggies, everyone skimps on the latter. The problem is mainly that dried veggies are simply less available than dried fruits. To solve for this, stock your pantry online. I recommend things like Karen's Naturals dried veggies and Mother Earth freeze dried broccoli. At the grocery store, you can usually find wasabi peas, seasoned dried chickpeas, or veggie chips, or kale chips (too crumbly for snacking, add into dinners).

#9: Too bland

If you cook your own breakfasts or dinners, there's probably room to add more flavor and ingredients to spice things up. Here are a few of my favorite additives: olive oil packets, sriracha packets, jerk seasoning, salt and pepper, dried veggies, cheese, bacon bits, salami, pepperoni, summer sausage (or flavored soy protein if you're vegetarian).

Mistake #10: Too expensive

Let's be honest, backpacking gear is expensive enough already. Nobody wants to break the bank on food. The easiest ways to cut costs are buying in bulk and avoiding particularly expensive foods like freeze dried meals, jerky (always overpriced and not high in calories), and the archetypical chia-based energy bars. Instead of buying individual bars, buy six packs. Instead of buying jerky, buy summer sausage. Instead of freeze dried meals, eat couscous, mashed potatoes, ramen, or stove-top stuffing. Backpacking food doesn't need to be expensive! $20 per day is a reasonable target.

Behind only hiking and sleeping, eating is the third most common ways to spend time on a backpacking trip, so it pays oodles of lifetime value to master the art. Are you an aspiring backcountry gourmand? Then the challenge of packing delicious lightweight food should inspire you to keep perfecting a menu. Do you view food purely as fuel? Then finding the most calorically dense options will certainly appeal. No matter your style, there's lots to be gained in upgrading your pantry. Happy hiking!

Conclusion

People pack heavy, because they pack for their fears—for their wildly imagined "what if the worst happens scenarios." Rather than relying on their camping skills (which should be more than adequate) and the predicted weather and conditions for their hike, they choose to overcompensate for their fears by packing heavy, over-kill gear, extra clothes, extra food etc. But heavy packing doesn't make you all that much safer, warmer, well fed or comfortable. It just makes your pack heavy and walking slow and unpleasant. So try backpacking ultralight…

Manufactured by Amazon.ca
Bolton, ON